AWS CERTII
CLOUD PRACTITIONER
CERTIFICATION GUIDE:

NEVILLE DAWSON

Table of Contents

INTRODUCTION

A WS - Amazon Web Services is one of the most complete and widely distributed cloud platforms globally. You can get more than 175 fully-featured services at different data centers worldwide. There are many clients of various rapidly developing start-ups, large companies, and government organizations. AWS helps these customers save costs, make the concept more flexible, and modernize quickly.

Origin of AWS Services

In 2002, the AWS platform was launched. In tit early stage, AWS offered only a few tools and services. It was up until March 14, 2006, when AWS was officially re-launched, combining the three initial service offerings of Amazon EC2, SQS, and S3 cloud storage. Amazon launched IT services in the form of web services that have brought them to the spotlight of cloud computing in recent years. In typical scenarios, we have to pay for servers and other IT infrastructures, but with Amazon Web Services, we pay for what we use. Every second it runs on a thousand servers simultaneously, which will produce faster results.

AWS products include services such as security, analytics, development tools, databases, archiving, networking, migration, and business applications. These services are distributed on the go with a pricing model.

AWS is a subsidiary of Amazon.com, which offers cloud computing services at very reasonable prices suitable for small businesses. Previously, when companies used their personal resources to store or calculate instances, a global solution was needed where you did not have to buy resources every time, but anyone can always do it.

Now, most companies prefer to move their data to the cloud to improve performance and also eliminate backup problems.

Here are statistics to help you apprehend why using AWS is necessary for IT professionals around the world:

- Cloud computing will grow to 150 billion USD by 2020 or more.
- Experts predict millions of jobs in the cloud.
- Cloud adoption has increased revenue by at least 40% or more in recent years.
- Based on these Gartner of Forbes statistics, it is clear that AWS is the latest trend in the IT sector and is expected to grow in the near future.

Advantages of AWS
Convenient

Payments can only be made for storage, computing power, and other resources without simple obligations or long-term contracts. The pricing model for Amazon Web Service is "pay for what you use."

Flexibility

The entire process and workflow for receiving AWS services are quite simple and straightforward. This kind of simple procedure is only thanks to AWS programs, operating systems, software architecture, and databases. As an IT, you can be confident that you can achieve a seamless transition by restructuring or migrating your IT infrastructure.

Simple setup

For setup, the subscription and AWS process takes no more than a day. An uninterrupted locale is not required for deployment because AWS is cloud-based. It has complete documentation to run virtual servers, and therefore, developers can configure programs from the preparatory stage to implementation with highly efficient programs.

Security

Amazon provides many justifications to guarantee the highest data security values. You can see a non-cooperative service at the time of the emergency or when we can see a trigger in the BCP (Business Continuity Plan).

API

Various programming languages are used in the API, which can be useful for systematic infrastructure management. Thanks to the API, you can start a new copy or organize your backups. APIs are also more powerful than the AWS Management Console.

AWS Main Services

From app analysis to development, Amazon offers a variety of useful services. The following are some of the basic components of the AWS atmosphere, and I will explain to them to let you know why each of these services is very important.

AWS Route 53

This is a highly accessible, mountable Domain Name System (DNS) service. The AWS Route 53 can be used to carry out the three primary functions of integrity checking, DNS routing, and domain registration. These are functions that can be carried out in any combination, but if you must carry out these functions via Route 53, it is required that you follow the steps in order.

A website always needs a name, like amazon.com. Therefore, registering the domain name is the first step. Once the domain name has been defined, it is necessary to connect the website to the browser via route 53, and this is where DNS routing is performed in the second step. The last step is to check the status of your sources. Automated requests are routed from Route 53 to your health verification sources, such as availability, functionality, and accessibility. You are also authorized to choose a notification if a resource is unavailable for any reason.

Amazon EC2

Amazon EC2 - Amazon Elastic Compute Cloud is responsible for computing. These are virtual servers called instances with high computing power. It provides an automatic resizing tool to change capacity dynamically. EC2 container log and EC2 allow clients to work with containers and Docker images on the AWS platform.

EC2 is also helpful for server hosting and setup process. With Amazon EC2, it becomes very easy to distribute your server. The EC2 is a powerful web service that is secure, customizable with high computing capacity in the cloud. This simple web services interface permits you to acquire and develop capacity with a nominal force. Get full control of IT assets, and you can work in the IT environment configured by Amazon.

The economy can be changed from Amazon EC2 by simply paying for the capacity actually used. To create robust applications in case of failure and isolated from public failures, Amazon EC2 has many tools available to developers. The virtual computing environment on AWS is called Instances. You can install and configure the application and the operating system running on the instance.

Amazon S3

Amazon S3 – Amazon Simple Storage Service Storage provides a rigid storage service for analysis and data backup. Each file is stored as objects here. An IT professional can store up to 3 GB in these Amazon S3 graphics to manage them properly. In the case of companies, Amazon glacier can store data similar to cold storage in the long term. Another service that offers cloud-based file storage is Amazon Elastic Block Store.

Amazon S3 is a great feature for moving and storing data. We need scalable storage to create a dominant cloud, to move and store data around the world effortlessly, and Amazon S3 can provide all the necessary tools with compartments. You can designate containers on AWS in four different ways: Amazon Reduced Redundancy Storage, Amazon Infrequent Access Storage, Amazon Glacier, and Amazon Standard Storage.

AWS CloudWatch

This is useful for monitoring services in your AWS surrounding. You can easily monitor important resources like Amazon EC2 instance, Amazon RDS DB instances, Amazon DynamoDB tables, and custom statistics generated by your apps and services. By collecting logs through this process, you get a clear picture of all AWS components.

AWS CloudFront

When it comes to delivering content for a reasonable price and at a faster rate, then AWS CloudFront comes into play. AWS CloudFront is a global content delivery system that brings content closer to users, just as the AWS region delivers it.

AWS ELB

Amazon has an AWS-mountable, authorized load balancing function called Amazon Elastic Load Balancer (Amazon ELB). If you want to send client requests to the correct servers and avoid all available access points, ELB plays an important role. I hope you know that we only have to pay for the services we use. In this case, we must make the ELB payment based on the time and the amount of data processed.

In addition to the main AWS services mentioned above, few services are optional for AWS users to enhance the cloud ecosystem.

- CloudTrail: The AWS CloudTrail is suitable for logging important information such as time of events, source IP address, transactions, and some others.
- AWS Configuration - With AWS Configuration, you can view your AWS infrastructure with care and remain moderate and secure.
- Lambda: AWS Lambda extracts the core AWS infrastructure and allows the developers to pay more attention when executing code.

Manage AWS services

Amazon web service is truly an on-demand cloud computing platform that provides a flexible, reliable, scalable, managed, easy-to-use, and affordable cloud computing solution, all of which have a different level of abstraction, such as IaaS, PaaS, and SaaS; all services can be used for a fee, to pay only for what is used and when IT resources are used.

It is easy to resize as needed. Servers are distributed worldwide and are therefore easily accessible, and the data stored on these servers is easy to retrieve. It is safe and reliable. Today AWS is widely used and preferred as a cloud service provider. It offers more than 100 services, including IT, storage, management tools, analytics, deployment, IoT, and more. All of these services are provided on the Amazon portal based on the user's subscription. Most of these services are available as HTTP calls using the SOAP protocol.

List Of Services Offered By AWS
Analytics

Analytics has always been an important basis of growth for companies. Data is always evaluated because it provides valuable information. Clients want or perhaps need a system that is not only scalable but fast enough to handle large amounts of data and provide useful information. AWS offers several applications for this. The Amazon

EMR delivers the Hadoop framework for big data processing. The Amazon Kinesis helps analyze data transmission in real-time. Amazon Data Pipeline and Glue gives pipeline structures that schedule loading and data processing. AWS offers many other applications for almost all operations.

Storage

We all know that data must be stored somewhere to process it. Amazon web services offer Storage in three main categories: block, object, and file storage. Amazon Glacier provides storage space for archived data and convenient recovery. Amazon S3 provides scalable data storage with backup and replication. AWS Backup Service automates the backup processes and manages data backup. In addition to these applications, Amazon web service storage offers other services.

Compute

Computing is necessary to manage every organization. From hosting web applications to performing certain functions in a serverless environment, computing is fundamental. Amazon web services provide a full range of IT services like Amazon EC2 and provides virtual servers or instances for IT professionals. It can be updated automatically as per requirement. AWS Lambda offers serverless processing to run applications. Amazon ECS is a high-quality container service that supports Docker containers. Lightsail is an intuitive service that provides storage space, virtual server, DNS management, etc. It also offers all the needed services for the development of applications.

DEMYSTIFICATION OF THE CLOUD COMPUTING BASE

What Is Cloud Computing?

To get started with AWS, there are a few basic concepts that a person should know.

Cloud Computing Concepts

Cloud computing is the process of utilizing a network of servers that are remotely hosted on the internet in place of using locally hosted servers or a local system to manage, store, process, and share data or resources.

Cloud computing uses the cloud a provider, which means:

- That the cloud provider is responsible for the hiring of IT staff to manage and run the systems.
- That the cloud provider is responsible for renting or owning the property where the data centers are housed.
- The cloud provider is responsible for all the risks associated with running, managing, and maintaining systems.
- That the customer is only responsible for configuring and maintaining their cloud or any code used by them.
- On-premise computing means:
- That an organization owns or leases its equipment which includes

servers and other networking systems.

- That an organization is responsible for the hiring of its IT staff to manage, run, and maintain the on-premise systems.
- That an organization takes on all the risks involved with the running, maintenance, and management of the on-premise systems.
- That any data centers or buildings housing the on-premise systems are owned, rented, or leased by an organization.

Large corporations tend to have on-premise computing systems, although some are finding it beneficial to move some if not all of their systems to cloud-based computing systems. For small to medium-sized businesses, cloud computing has its benefits and offers greater opportunities for better and more advanced systems that are cost-effective.

The Advantages of Cloud Computing

There are many advantages and benefits for businesses as well as individuals to use cloud computing services.

These advantages and benefits include:

On-Demand Resources

Instead of investing in on-premise solutions that can cost a fortune for the initial outlay, cloud services allow for pay-on demand services. This means that the cost of buying expensive servers and software to run on the servers is completely cut out. The facility allows customers to get what they want when they want without having to wait for resources.

Pay as You Go

With on-demand resources, the customer is only paying for what they need or use. This eliminates long-term commitments and allows for resources that the company no longer needs to do away with the resources.

When IT managers scope out systems, they do so by calculating how much data on average the organization uses over a span of two years or so.

With that in mind, they need to estimate as to what a system will require to incorporate company growth for the next few years. As data usage within an organization can grow, stagnate, or even slow down, this is mostly prediction analysis. With cloud computing, there is no more guesswork or having to upgrade the system every two years or so to ensure the company does not run out of space. With cloud computing services, there is no paying for underutilized capacity or running out of capacity; the system can be scaled up or down as or when required.

Cost Sharing

Because other customers are using cloud services, cloud service providers can offer better deals to their customers. In essence, this means that you are sharing the cost of data centers, software, and resources with other users of the cloud.

Greater Agility and Increased Speed

Not only can you scale solutions on-demand, but any new software roll-outs or upgrades can be done from one central location.

No More Data Center Costs

Cut down on expensive data centers or regulation server rooms. This allows for an organization to invest more on desktop systems rather than expensive server solutions.

Managed Services

AWS offers managed services, which frees an organization up to use the tool instead of having the operational burdens of managing the tools.

Expand Nationally or Globally

Expanding globally or nationally no longer requires having to invest in expensive resources. Organizations can now run their applications(s) from the cloud, enabling their staff to work from anywhere in the world with ease.

AWS Value Propositions

The advantages of implementing AWS offer the customer the following benefits:

- OpEx over CapEx means that there are more cash flow and a better bottom line for the customer.
- Agility and flexibility allowing for on-demand resources that are not readily available for on-premise systems. It also gives the customer more choice of applications or systems that was not possible in an on-premise system environment.
- Scalability is fast and can be done in a matter of minutes saving time, resources, and money. This elasticity gives customers room for growth that on-premise systems may have either a limit to or is too costly.
- Time to market is decreased due to not having lengthy system roll-outs, getting large budgets passed for the cost of equipment, resources, etc.
- Security of the AWS Cloud computing system gives customers peace of mind. There is no need for large backup centers; it eliminates downtime, and off-site disaster recovery centers.

The Different Types Of Cloud Computing

There are various types of cloud computing available for use. These are chosen depending on the organization's needs.

Types of cloud computing include:

Software as a Service (SaaS)

Software as a Service is customer orientated services that provide software that is a whole product. In other words, it does not need any tweaks or developing; it works and is maintained by the provider of the service.

Some examples of SaaS include; Gmail, Salesforce, Google Apps,

Zendesk, DocuSign, Dropbox, Slack, Monday.com, and MS Office 365.

Platform as a Service (PaaS)

Platform as a Service provides fully managed and maintained infrastructure for developers. The service provider will provide the hardware and already installed software so developers can concentrate on the development and deployment of their applications.

Some examples of PaaS include; Microsoft, Google, IBM, AWS, Red Hat, Pivotal, Oracle, Heroku, Mendix, AWS Elastic Beanstalk, and Engine Yard.

Infrastructure as a Service (IaaS)

Infrastructure as a Service is the infrastructure backbone that provides scalable solutions to meet customers' cloud computing needs. This is where storage solutions, processing services, and computers are provided for a customer's use. IaaS targets IT, administrative users, as a basic to more advanced knowledge in IT is needed to manage these services.

Services offered with IaaS can include; firewalls, auto-scaling, load balancers, monitoring, computing, databases, storage, content delivery networks, and more.

Some examples of IaaS include; Microsoft Azure, Google Cloud Platform, and AWS.

Deployment Methods for Cloud Computing

There are a few basic methods of deployment for cloud computing, which include the following.

Public Cloud

The public cloud is the most widely used cloud and is the cloud that most people think of when the term cloud computing is mentioned. This is where everything that is used is owned, managed, and run by a third party. Here all the resources and services are provided over the public internet and are the cheapest of all deployment methods as it is paid on a per user basis.

The downfall of this deployment method is that it leaves an establishment or person totally reliant on the third party for its services. If the third party has an outage or interruption, it is going to affect these services.

An example of this deployment method would include DropBox, Google Drive, Square Space, BaseCamp, and Slack.

This is the best platform to use for internet-based companies, start-ups, and is the basis for SaaS offerings.

Private Cloud

A private cloud is usually intranet-based, which means the only way to gain access to it is through the company network or a VPN application.

Although this type of cloud solution is just as flexible as the public cloud and offers the same sort of benefits as the public cloud, it is more secure. Access is limited to a company or person with user access to it.

The major downfall of a private cloud is the cost of the cloud solution, and as such, it is mostly used by large corporations or companies with the budget for it.

Community Cloud

The community cloud is much like the public cloud mixed with the private cloud. This type of deployment method allows for software and systems to be maintained by the service provider with shared resources between several organizations. The community cloud can be either maintained independently by the organization or the cloud provider. This type of cloud deployment is flexible, scalable, and offers the benefits of shared licenses, software, and other computing resources.

Although not nearly as expensive as the private cloud deployment method, the community cloud method can still be quite expensive to maintain. This deployment method best suits organizations such as manufacturing and financial institutes.

Hybrid Cloud

The hybrid cloud deployment method is one that can combine on-premise computing with one of the above cloud computing deployment methods. Or it can be the combination of the deployment mentioned above methods.

Although this method can get messy in that it can create inconsistencies when it comes to the adherence of company policies, upgrades, maintenance, or software, a lot of larger corporations finds it effective. This kind of deployment method allows for an organization to have flexible, scalable solutions that meet it's software and system needs. They can also keep their more sensitive data on-site and secure it on their premises.

AWS Global Infrastructure

To give AWS customers the most streamlined service that allows for a higher throughput while maintaining a lower latency, Amazon continues to expand its global reach.

You can see the AWS Global Infrastructure at the following website link:

https://www.infrastructure.aws/

AWS Global Infrastructure is broken into:

Regions

As of the publishing of this guide, AWS could be found in 24 launched geographic locations around the globe. The region is where AWS is physically located around the world. Each region is a completely independent entity to any other region.

Each geographical region will have at least two independent data centers (availability zones or AZs) with the largest of the regions being North Virginia or the US-East.

WHAT IS AWS CERTIFICATION?

With AWS certification, cloud experts can train professionals to improve their required skills and help companies create innovative and effective cloud initiative teams with AWS. It offers various roles and specialty certification exams designed to enable the respective teams and individuals to achieve their unique goals.

List Of AWS Certification

The following are several role-based certifications:

- Cloud practioner
- Architect
- Developer
- Operations
- Engineers
- Administrator

IT professionals earn AWS certification to demonstrate and validate technical knowledge and skills in the cloud.

Why Is AWS Certification Important?

All organizations like to move their legacy applications, infrastructures, and systems to the cloud, regardless of size. Therefore, there is a high demand for cloud computing professionals in the sector. In this huge market for cloud services, Amazon Web Services has a majority stake and offers many advantages. Benefits can help cloud professionals take advantage of AWS career opportunities. Obtaining an AWS certificate offers the following benefits:

Digital badge

Show your certification with a digital badge on your social media and electronic signatures. You also get instant access to AWS sponsored certification events.

Research presentation

Get access to a 50% coupon to request a new certification or another exam.

Recognition of the event.

Receive invitations to regional recognition receptions and use your digital badge to gain exclusive access to AWS certification rooms to reinvent and select AWS Summit events.

AWS Certified Global Community

Access the LinkedIn community and AWS-certified network with your colleagues.

Free training exams

Prepare for your AWS certification with a good practice exam.

AWS certified store

Unlock access to exclusive AWS certified products.

Why choose AWS certification?

Cloud adoption statistics show that cloud technology is the future.

Cloud technologies are quickly becoming the future of organizations in many sectors. The emergence of advanced technologies such as artificial intelligence (AI) and machine learning is driving cloud technology. According to a Forbes article from 2018, 83% of corporate workloads will be in the cloud by 2020. This is an amazing forecast. Gaining experience in the field of cloud computing will soon is a must for IT professionals.

AWS is the undisputed leader in the IAAS cloud computing market

A recent article by Gartner, the leading research and consulting firm, analyzed that the global infrastructure as a service (IAAS) market grew by 29.5% in 2017, showing that cloud adoption organizations are on the rise. The same report found that Amazon Web Services (AWS) owned 53.7% of this IAAS market.

Obtaining a certification distinguishes your CV from other qualified candidates.

With the annual growth in the cloud industry, many will need to learn AWS technology to keep up with industry changes and remain relevant in their work. Being certified now can take it a step further in a fast-growing market.

AWS Certification Offers Well-Paid Jobs

Among current IT certifications, AWS certifications are at the top of the most profitable certifications. Based on a ranking of the most popular certifications in the IT industry, AWS Certified Developer - Associate is fourth on the list of most profitable certifications.

AWS certification is a viable goal

Since AWS certification has been around in one form or another since 2013, there are many resources available to help prospective test candidates learn AWS.

Often the best AWS training offers a combination of theory with great hands-on exposure to core platform services. The wealth of information available, sample questions, and best practices available make certification a real possibility.

Specialized tracks help you develop your current career and field of expertise on the platform.

Once you start discovering AWS services and becoming certified, the journey doesn't have to end there. Amazon has introduced AWS Network and Security Specialization Certifications to help you maintain your advanced skills and allow you to learn new aspects of the platform. To pass one of the specialty exams, you must take one of the main associated exams.

With AWS certifications, you qualify for the professional program.

AWS has a Professional Program (EMS) for qualified and certified individuals. As an SME, you can attend various seminars and help with the exam development process.

An AWS certification demonstrates your credibility and competence with potential clients.

When working in a customer role or offering AWS-related technologies to potential customers, trust and credibility are important factors in building and maintaining relationships. Customers often want to know that they are dealing with IT experts who interest or want to adopt them.

AWS Certifications Open Organizations to Partner Program Benefits

When organizations have multiple AWS-certified employees in the organization, companies can take advantage of different levels of the AWS Partner Program. The AWS Partner Program enables qualified organizations to obtain AWS Partner Designation. This allows organizations to access a variety of resources and training to better support their customers when they work with AWS services.

Organizations enjoy greater benefits at all levels of the partner program. The more certified an organization is, the more benefits it will receive.

Amazon also offers you the official use of the AWS certified logo and digital badges so you can see your credentials worldwide.

In summary, AWS has become one of the fastest-growing IT products in the field of information technology. Businesses are driving incredible speeds with AWS. By getting AWS certified right away, you can gain the necessary knowledge and learn the tools necessary to work in this new technology landscape.

AWS CERTIFIED CLOUD PRACTITIONER

The AWS Cloud Practitioner Certification Exam (CLF-C01) is designed for individuals who have the knowledge and skills to effectively demonstrate a complete understanding of the AWS Cloud, regardless of the specific technical roles covered by other AWS certifications.

Applicants can be business analysts, project managers, experienced managers, AWS Academy students, and other IT professionals.

The Cloud Practitioner certification exam is a pass or failed exam. The Cloud Practitioner exam is assessed by a minimum standard set by AWS professionals, guided by best practices and guidelines in the certification industry. Test results are reported as a score of 100-1000, with a minimum passing score of 700. The score shows how well you have passed the test as a whole. Total passing scores allow you to compare scores between different versions of the same exam.

AWS Cloud Definition

AWS Cloud offers a wide range of infrastructure services (more than 50 services available), such as processing power, storage options, networks, and databases, provided as a tool: request, available in seconds, with payment based on price. It is available with forty-four Availability Zones in 16 geographic regions worldwide, with 17 additional Availability

Zones and six other announced regions.

AWS's extensive security certification and accreditation, encryption of data at rest and on the move, hardware security modules, and enhanced physical security contribute to a more secure way of managing your organization's IT infrastructure. With AWS cloud, identity control, configuration, and usage, control, and management capabilities are integrated into the platform to help you meet compliance and governance requirements. Ultimately, most of the value will be in the architecture of native cloud technologies, rather than an increase and change in the existing data center. Let's take a quick look at the benefit of cloud computing from an IT perspective:

- Trade Your Capital Expenses For Variable Expenses

Instead of capitalizing heavily in data centers and servers before you know how to use them, you can only pay if you use computing resources and not just the amount you consume.

- Stop Guessing Capacity

Take the guesswork out of your infrastructure's capacity needs. When making a capacity decision before deploying an application, you often run expensive idle or limited capacity resources. These problems go away from cloud computing. You can access all the capacity you want and scale in minutes.

- Increase Speed And Agility

When it comes to the cloud computing ecosystem, new IT resources are just a click away, meaning you can shorten the time developer resources are available from weeks to weeks. This results in a dramatic increase in organization agility, as the costs and time required to experiment and develop significantly lower.

- Stop spending money on data center management and maintenance.

Focus on projects that set your business apart, not infrastructure. .

- Go Global In Minutes

Quickly and easily deploy your app to various regions of the world with just a few clicks. This means that you can offer your customers less latency and a better experience at a minimal cost.

- Identify aspects of the AWS cloud economy.

Your organization is most likely not responsible for managing the data centers, but it takes a lot of time and money. Amazon Web Services offers a way to buy and use infrastructure on-demand, so you only pay for what you use.

- Prices While You Work

AWS does not require minimum cost commitments or long-term contracts. Replace high up-front costs with low variable payments that only apply to what you use. With AWS, you are not subject to multi-year agreements or complex licensing models.

- Progressive Pricing (Use More, Pay Less)

AWS follows a differentiated pricing model for data storage and transfer. The more you use storage and data transfer, the less you pay per gigabyte. Plus, volume discounts and custom pricing are available for high-volume projects with unique requirements.

- Cost Optimization

Cost optimization is a free tool that provides pre-configured reports for AWS current expense inquiries for current and historical periods, as well as forecasts. You can also customize the reports to your specific needs or download the billing data to use with your tools.

- Trusted Advisor

The Trusted Advisor inspects your AWS environment to find opportunities that can save you money, improve system performance, increase the reliability of your applications, and help you implement security best practices. Since 2013, clients have seen more than 2.6 million best practice recommendations and have achieved more than $ 350 million in estimated savings.

Architecture Design Principles

This framework offers customers and partners a consistent approach to evaluating architectures and provides advice to help implement projects that will evolve over time based on the needs of your application.

- Security

The ability to protect information, systems, and resources while providing corporate value through risk assessments and mitigation strategies. The security pillar focuses on protecting information and systems. Key topics include privacy and data integrity, identifying and managing who can do what with privilege management, system protection, and setting controls to detect security events.

- Reliability

The system's ability to recover from an infrastructure or service failure, dynamically acquire IT resources to meet demand and reduce interruptions such as configuration errors or temporary network problems.

The pillar of reliability aims to prevent malfunctions and quickly repair malfunctions to meet the demand of companies and customers. Key topics include configuration basics, cross-project requirements, recovery planning, and how we manage change.

- Operational Excellence

The capacity to run and monitor systems to deliver business value and continually improve support processes and procedures.

The pillar of operational excellence focuses on the operation and monitoring of systems to offer commercial value and continuous improvement of processes and procedures. Key topics include managing and automating change, responding to events, and setting standards to manage daily operations successfully.

These principles will be described in more detail below.

- Fundamentals
- Scalability
- Disposable fonts instead of fixed servers
- Automation
- Loose coupling
- Services, not servers
- Databases
- Manage the increase in data volumes.
- Eliminate some points of failure
- Optimize for costs
- Caching
- Protection

The following sections provide details:

- Scalability

Elasticity and scalability are two fundamental principles of cloud architecture that guide the AWS architecture.

Elasticity is the ability to use resources dynamically and efficiently to avoid the traditional model against an oversupply of infrastructure resources to meet capacity needs. Significantly, elasticity avoids the cost of these overloaded resources, such as energy, space, and maintenance. This is AWS "pay as you go" or "pay for what you use."

Scalability is the ability to evolve without changing the design. With AWS, scalability is achieved through scalability. The infrastructure and components of the application are based on the assumption that they will fail, rather than relying solely on high availability. The technological components are basic elements that can be thrown away if they fail and grow, adding more if desired. A guiding principle is a consistent approach to architecture and growth.

There are two types of scaling:

- Horizontal scaling: increase in the number of fonts. Automatic scaling and priming are used for the horizontal scale. Auto Scale allows you to automatically resize horizontally to fit the load. The startup allows you to configure servers after startup automatically. (Using components like Amazon Machine Images (AMI) and CloudFormation to automate).

Vertical scaling: increased resource capacity (for example, faster processor, more memory, and more storage space).

Available resources

Resources should be treated as temporarily available resources rather than on-site fixed assets.

AWS focuses on the concept of undisputable organization: a started server never updates during its life cycle. Updates can be done on a new server with the latest configuration. This ensures that resources are always consistent (and tested) and that they are easier to recover.

AWS offers several ways to create instances of computing resources in an automated and reproducible way:

- Bootstrap: scripts to configure and install, for example using data scripts and cloud in it to install software or copy fonts and code

- Containers: AWS support for Docker images via Elastic Beanstalk and ECS. Docker allows you to group the software into a Docker image, a standardized software development unit that contains everything the software needs to do: code, runtime, system tools, system libraries, etc.
- Infrastructure as code: AWS resources are programmable. Software development techniques, practices, and tools can be applied to make the entire infrastructure reusable, maintainable, extensible, and verifiable. AWS offers services like CloudFormation and OpsWorks to encrypt deployment.

- Automation

Unlike traditional IT infrastructure, the cloud enables automation of numerous events, improving both the stability of the system and the efficiency of your organization. Some of the AWS resources that can be used for automation are:

- AWS Elastic Beanstalk - This resource is the fastest and easiest way to run an application on AWS. You can simply download your application code and the service will automatically manage all the details, such as resource provisioning, load balancing, auto escalation, and monitoring.
- Amazon EC2 Auto Recovery: You can build an Amazon CloudWatch alarm that will monitor an Amazon EC2 instance and automatically recover it in case of damage. Note, however, that when the instance is restored, the instance is migrated through a restart of the instance, and all data in memory is lost.
- Automatic resizing - Automatic resizing allows you to maintain application availability and automatically increase or decrease Amazon EC2 capacity based on defined conditions.
- Amazon CloudWatch alarms: You can build a CloudWatch alarm that sends an Amazon Simple Notification Service (Amazon SNS) message when a certain measurement exceeds a specified threshold

for a specified number of periods.

EXAM PREPARATIONS

Essential Things to Remember Before Your Exam

In the way of summary, let's quickly run down the key things you need to remember before taking the exam, including sample questions on each topic.

Storage And Database Section

The main storage options available in AWS are:

- Amazon Instance store
- Amazon Simple Storage Service (S3) and Glacier for archiving
- Elastic Level Storage
- Elastic file systems
- Databases - Amazon relational databases (RDS), Amazon DynamoDB, Amazon Aurora and Redshift.

Amazon S3

Amazon s3 is highly durable and available by itself. Amazon S3 guarantees 99.99% availability and 99.999999999% durability.

Cross-region replication can be enabled for S3 anytime, but if you already had some objects in a bucket when you enable the cross-region replication, only newly added objects will be replicated.

Another important thing to remember is versioning is a prerequisite for enabling Cross Regional replication.

There will be at least two questions in the exam based on the lifecycle policy. To respond to these laid out questions, you will need to know the difference between s3 standard, S3 standard infrequent access, and S3 Glacier.

S3 standard is for general purpose storage for frequently accessed data.

On the other hand, S3 standard IA is suitable for infrequently accessed files that require rapid access when needed. It is cheaper than the S3 standard.

Amazon Glacier

Glacier is the cheapest storage option, and it is used for archiving data for seven to ten years or longer to meet regulatory compliance or requirements for some organizations.

The normal retrieval time for glacial storage is within 12 hours; it's not instant. But there are options available for an expedited retrieval with an extra fee and which will be in minutes.

When we talk about Amazon glacier, another important point to remember is unlike s3, you won't be able to upload an object to Glacier directly from the console. But we can use API or lifecycle policies to put that into glacier.

There are two more storage types available in S3 which are:

- S3 One Zone Infrequent access storage and
- S3 glacier deep archive

Sample questions:

A marketing company needs to upload videos, and these are accessed frequently for the first 30 days, then it is accessed only once in a while. After 12 months, the video will never be accessed but will need it for auditing purposes. What is the best option in the scenario?

Explanation:

Here the video is accessed frequently for the first 30 days, which means it should be stored in Amazon s3 standard for 30 days. Then it is accessed only once in a while, so it means it can be moved to Amazon s3 infrequent storage. After 12 months, the video will never be accessed, that means you can move that video to Glacier, which is still available for auditing purposes.

Correct answer:

1. Store videos in S3 standard and set a lifecycle policy to move to s3 standard IA after 30 days, then move to glacier after 12 months.
2. A travel website is using S3 is to store high-definition images uploaded by their clients. You have noticed the images from the S3 buckets are used on third-party blogs and websites using the URL.

As a solution architect how will you stop this?

Explanation:

In S3, there is an option to use pre-signed a URL to avoid unwanted access to the website images shared using the web link. The pre-signed URLs are valid only for a specific duration. In the actual examination, you can expect a question with a similar sort of idea.

Another thing is origin access identity (OAI), which is used to maintain secure access to the files in s3 that you serve through CloudFront.

CloudFront is a fast content delivery network to improve website latency. It securely delivers data, videos, and applications from the closest 'points of presence.'

AWS Athena And AWS Glue

Amazon Athena is an interactive clearing service that makes it easy to analyze data in Amazon s3 using standard C code. Most results are delivered within seconds.

Amazon Glue is a fully managed extract, transform, and load (ETL) service that makes it easier for clients to get ready and load their data to analysis software.

A point to note for the exam is that Athena is always integrated with AWS Glue.

Athena is integrated with AWS Glue to make an easy data analysis tool.

Block Level Storage - Ebs

The key idea to remember is the difference between all of the EBS volume types.

I have highlighted some points in red (in the image below) for your reference.

Amazon EBS volume types

The following table shows use cases and performance characteristics of current generation EBS volumes:

Volume Type	Solid State Drives (SSD)		Hard Disk Drives (HDD)	
	EBS Provisioned IOPS SSD (io1)	EBS General Purpose SSD (gp2)	Throughput Optimized HDD (st1)	Cold HDD (sc1)
Use Cases	I/O-intensive NoSQL and relational databases	Boot volumes, low-latency interactive apps, dev & test	Big data, data warehouses, log processing	Colder data requiring fewer scans per day
Volume Size	4 GB - 16 TB	1 GB - 16 TB	500 GB - 16 TB	500 GB - 16 TB
Max IOPS/Volume	64,000	16,000	500	250
Max Throughput/Volume	1,000 MB/s	250 MB/s	500 MB/s	250 MB/s
Max IOPS/Instance	80,000	80,000	80,000	80,000
Max Throughput/Instance	1,750 MB/s	1,750 MB/s	1,750 MB/s	1,750 MB/s

There are four types of Amazon EBS volume:

- EBS provisioned IOPS SSD (io1)
- EBS general purpose SSD (gp2)
- Throughput optimized HDD (st 1) and

- Cold HDD (sc1)

Try to remember the short code for each volume types. For example, EBS provisioned IOPS SSD is iO1.

Throughput optimized HDD is st 1.

The first thing to note is the use cases of each of the volume types.

- EBS provision IOPS SSD is used for I/O-intensive workloads such as NoSQL, DynamoDB and relational databases.
- EBS general-purpose SSD is bit cheaper than the previous one. It is mainly used for low latency interactive applications.
- Both of the HDD options are basically used for data warehousing and archiving respectively.

Another thing to remember is the maximum IOPS per volume for EBS provision iOPs SSD and EBS general purpose SSD.

For EBS provision iOPs SSD, the maximum IOPS per volume is 64,000 whereas in EBS general-purpose SSD is 16,000.

Sample questions:

1. You are setting up a cost-operational architecture for an application that has intensive workloads that require 42,000 iOPs. The application should be hosted in an on-demand EC2 instance in your VPC.

What is the most suitable EBS volume type to use with the scenario?

Explanation:

The answer is iO1 because it is the iOPS optimized EBS volume, and it can give up to 64,000 iOPS per volume.

You can expect a similar sort of questions in your exam.

Ebs

EBS is highly durable and available in a region, but if that region fails, the data is lost. This is because it's not replicating between the regions.

Key point: You can't enable cross-region replication in EBS, but the only way is to create a snapshot and copy to another region manually.

Efs

EFS is a simple, scalable, fully managed elastic file system which can be used with all the AWS cloud services and on-premise resources. It is built to scale to petabytes without disrupting the application.

One EFS can connect to multiple services.

Rds

RDS is a relational database sitting in the cloud.

Six familiar database engines to choose from – Amazon Aurora, PostgreSQL, MySQL, MariaDB, Oracle Database, and SQL Server.

RDS is used when the database is having Schema, joins, etc. To make RDS highly available, multi availability zone (multi-AZ) feature can be enabled.

Amazon Aurora

Amazon Aurora is a MySQL and PostgreSQL-compatible relational database. Amazon Aurora is five times faster than the standard MySQL database and three times faster than the standard PostgreSQL database.

Amazon Aurora replicates across three availability zone by default.

Read replicas to another region can be enabled for better performance, and the latency will be less than 100 milliseconds when it is enabled.

There will be questions regarding Amazon Aurora and the multi availability zone feature of RDS.

Sample questions:

1. An application is deployed in a fleet of spot EC2 instances and uses MySQL RDS database instance running in one availability zone. You need to ensure high availability and scalability.

Which option performs synchronous data replication in RDS?

Correct answer:

The answer is to "enable RDS database instance running in a multi availability zone deployment."

2. As a solutions architect, you have been requested to set up highly available application in AWS which the database must be in three availability zone. What can help you accomplish this goal?

Correct answer:

Only Amazon Aurora is capable to deploy in more than two availability zones.

Dynamo DB

Amazon DynamoDB is a reliable and flexible NoSQL database service offered by the AWS cloud. DynamoDB cannot be used if the database has some schemas and joins. It can support up to 20 million requests per second and ten trillion records per day.

Amazon Dynamo DB Accelerator (DAX) is an add-on service used to tune the DynamoDB for better performance.

Common use cases of DynamoDB:

- Database for shopping carts
- Storing JSON or CSV or any other structured data files
- Inventory tracking and fulfillment applications and

- Customer profiles and accounts databases

Sample Questions:

1. A game is using DynamoDB as the database and improving the game's performance, which AWS service can be used to reduce DynamoDB response times from milliseconds to microseconds?

Correct Answer:

The answer is DynamoDB accelerator (DAX) which can reduce the response times from milliseconds to microseconds.

2. Your supervisor has instructed you to set up a web application that can collect votes for a popular TV competition. Billions of users will submit votes and must be collected real-time and stored into a highly scalable and highly available database.

What is the best service you should use for this scenario?

Correct Answer:

Because this data is structured and without much-complicated schemas or joints DynamoDB is the perfect solution.

Ec2

Amazon Elastic Compute Cloud is a web service that provides secure, and resizable compute capacity in the cloud. EC2 is a crucial topic for the examination. You can expect questions based on the cost model and instance type.

It is essential to know how to select the instance type and the cost model based on the requirements. The comparison chart on the image below will give you a better idea about the cost models.

There are four types of a pricing model based on the capacity needs:

- On demand

- Reserved
- Spot instance and
- Dedicated instances

THE NEW SAA-C02 EXAM VERSION

The New Version Of The Saa-C02 Exam

The new SAA-C02 exam for the AWS Certified Solutions Architect Associate certification is available as of March 2020. The previous form of the exam was retired on July 1, 2020, after being extended for a few more months due to the closure of screening tests caused by the COVID-19 pandemic. It has been updated with new content to align with the latest AWS features and services.

To help you better prepare for the exam, let's take a look at the exam design and break down the different "domains" in the exam guide so you know what to expect.

Understand the AWS Exam Design.

This exam qualifies for membership in the AWS training program and is recommended for people with at least one year of practical experience.

The "AWS Certified Solutions Architect - Associate Exam Guide (SAA-C02)" recommends the following AWS skills:

- One year of hands-on experience designing scalable, fault-tolerant, accessible distributed systems available on AWS.
- Hands-on experience with AWS computer, networking, storage, and database services.

- Hands-on experience with AWS distribution and management services.
- Knowledge of the best practices recommended creating secure and reliable applications on the AWS platform.
- Understand the basic guidelines of the AWS cloud authoring architecture.
- Understanding of the global AWS infrastructure.
- Understanding of network technologies in relation to AWS.
- Understand the security features and tools provided by AWS and their relationship to traditional service

The exam includes 65 questions and has a time limit of 130 minutes. You must obtain a minimum score of 720 points out of 1000 to pass the exam.

The exam question format is one of the following:

- Multiple choice (one correct answer of four choices)
- Multiple choice (two or more correct answers of five or more choices)

Most questions are 1 to 2 lines of a scenario, followed by the question itself.

Important: Be very careful when reading the question text to make sure you select the correct answer! Sometimes it's easy to miss small details that change your answer, so don't rush your pass.

A. AWS SAA-CO2 Exam Question Allocation Table Content Outline

The exam has the following content domains that each make up a percentage of the exam:

Domain 1: Design Resilient Architectures, which makes up 30% of the exams.

This domain consists of the following topics or concepts for resilient

AWS architectures:

- The learner must be able to design a multi-tier architecture solution.
- The learner must be able to design highly available and fault-tolerant architectures.
- Using AWS service, the learner must be able to design decoupling mechanisms.
- The learning is required to know how to choose appropriate resilient storage.

Domain 2: Design High-Performing Architectures which makes up 28% of the exams.

This domain consists of the following topics or concepts pertaining to a workload:

- Identify scalable and elastic compute solutions for a workload.
- Select scalable and high-performing storage solutions for a workload.
- Select networking solutions based on high-performance for a workload.
- Select database solutions for a workload that is high-performance.

Domain 3: Design Secure Applications and Architectures, which makes up 24% of the exams.

This domain consists of the following topics or concepts about security:

- The learner must be able to design secure access to AWS resources.
- The learners must understand and be able to design secure application tiers.
- The learner must be confident enough to select appropriate data security options.

Domain 4: Design Cost-Optimized Architectures which makes up 18% of the exams.

This domain consists of the following topics or concepts about cost-optimization of AWS:

- This domain requires the student to be able to identify cost-effective storage solutions.
- The student must know how to identify database services and compute cost-effective services.
- The student must be able to expertly design cost-effective network architectures.

B. What to Expect From the Exam

To do well and pass the exam, the student is expected to know the AWS core services and use them to create systems that follow AWS best practices.

Every missed answer is marked as an incorrect answer, and an incorrect answer will bring down the overall score of the exam.

A question can be marked for future consideration, but try and guess what you think it may be before moving on to the next question. That way, if time runs out and you have not had a chance to go back to review the question, you have a chance of getting it right as opposed to not answering it at all.

After the exam, you can review each answer and questions you have marked for review. Marking a question for review also makes it easier to get back to, especially when running short.

It is vital to keep an eye on the time period throughout the exam, and if you feel you are spending too much time on a question, mark it for review rather than keep going back to it.

The exam content will contain questions that are broken down into

Response Types and **Unscored Content**.

When taking the exams, it is vital to remember that all the details on the test questions may count.

Response Types

The examination is broken down into two types of questions that will be asked of the student. These questions are:

- **Multiple choice questions**— These questions only have one correct answer, but the student will choose four answers to choose from. The three incorrect answers are what are known as distractor answers.

Example:

Q1: What is the shade of the sky?
C. Orange
D. Green
E. Azure
F. Lemon
Answer: C. Azure

- **Multiple response questions**—These types usually have one question with 5 to 6 answers to choose from. It will be stated how many correct answers to choose from the list of given answers. For instance, the question may say something like, from the following list, choose the two correct answers.

Example:

Q2: What are the parts of a motor car?
Choose two.
A. Seat
B. Jar

C. Engine

D. Lid

E. Bag

Answer: A. Seat & C. Engine

Not all of the questions will be ones that have obvious answers that stand out. Some of the questions will require the exam taker to choose the right procedure or solution for the scenario put forward in the matter.

Example:

Q3: Mary needs to make some toast with butter and jam. From the options below, choose the procedure that best explains how to make the buttered toast.

- A. Put the bread on the plate and butter it with fresh butter.
- B. Put the butter and bread on the plate with a knife.
- C. Put the bread and butter in the oven on high for 20 minutes.
- D. Put the bread in the toaster, and when it pops out, put it on a plate and butter the bread.

Answer: D. Put the bread in the toaster and when it pops out, put it on a plate and butter the bread.

Work through the questions by eliminating answers that you are sure do not pertain to the question. If you know the subject well enough, the incorrect answers will be clearer. There are always two answers that will look pretty similar. They need to be read through really carefully because this is what trips a student up.

Unscored Content

There may be what is called unscored content included on the exam. Although they do not affect the exam takers score they are there to gather statistical information.

End of the Exam

It is a good idea to flag questions you had doubts about, so if you have time after the exam, you can review them.

At the end of the exam, the student will receive their mark and whether or not they passed the exam. They will also get the statistics on what their strengths and weaknesses were for the subject based on answers.

Whether the learner passes or fails the exam, the strength and weakness table is a valuable tool. It will show the learner what they need to work on within the AWS domain to continue focusing on.

Do not feel down if you did not pass the first time around; not many people do. But you will know what you need to go back and work on to ensure you do pass the next time around.

VIRTUAL PRIVATE CLOUD (VPC)

Virtual private mists (VPCs) are anything, but difficult to-utilize AWS arranges coordinators and incredible devices for sorting out your framework. Since it's so natural to separate the occasions in one VPC from whatever else you have running, you should make another VPC for every single one of your undertakings or venture stages. For instance, you may have one VPC for early application improvement, another for beta testing, and a third for the generation (see Figure 2.1).

Tenancy

When propelling an EC2 example, you'll have the chance to pick a tenure model. The default setting is shared tenure, where your occasion will run as a virtual machine on a physical server that is simultaneously facilitating different examples. Those different cases likely could be claimed and worked by other AWS clients, in spite of the fact that the plausibility of any sort of uncertain cooperation between examples is remote.

To meet uncommon administrative prerequisites, your association's cases may require an additional degree of disconnection. The Dedicated Instance choice guarantees that your occurrence will run without anyone else committed physical server. This implies it won't be imparting the server to assets claimed by an alternate client account. The Dedicated Host alternative enables you to really recognize and control the physical server you've been appointed to meet progressively prohibitive authorizing or administrative prerequisites.

Normally, committed examples and devoted hosts will cost you more than occasions utilizing shared tenure. Exercise 2.1 will direct you through the dispatch of a basic EC2 Linux occurrence.

Choosing the right instance for your workload is essential to ensure the availability, scalability, and efficiency of your application. Amazon Web Services (AWS) offers several types of EC2 instances suitable for different sizes and purposes. But how to choose the best type of EC2 for your application? You need to know a little more about the subject to be able to choose more assertively.

T2, T3, M4, and M3: EC2 instances for conventional applications

For general purpose applications, these EC2 instances are the best choice, as they offer a balanced profile of computing, memory, and network resources.

T2 instances: recommended for medium-sized sites, web applications, and microservices.

T3 instances: update of T2 instances, with cost and performance advantages. They require minor changes to your configuration to work properly. They are also recommended for medium-sized sites, web applications, and microservices.

Configuring Instance Behavior

You can alternatively advise EC2 to execute directions on your occasion as it boots by highlighting client information in your case design (this is once in a while known as bootstrapping). Regardless of whether you determine the information during the support setup process or by utilizing the - client information esteem with the AWS CLI, you can have content records carry your occurrence to any ideal state.

Client information can comprise of a couple of straightforward directions to introduce a web server and populate its webroot, or it tends to be a modern content setting the occurrence up as a working hub inside a Puppet Enterprise–driven stage.

VPC sizing and structure.

How to size VPC

A subnet is in an availability zone. Try to divide each subnet into levels (application, web, database, reservation). Since each region has at least three AZs, it is good practice to start dividing the network into four different AZs. This allows at least one subnet in each AZ and one reservation. Taking a /16 subnet and dividing it into 16 shapes will make each one a /20.

Custom VPC

The custom VPC is an isolated and resistant regional service. It works from all the AZ in that region and allows isolated networks within AWS. No IN or OUT of a VPC without explicit configuration. We isolated explosion radio. Any issues are limited to that VPC or anything related to it. The custom VPC has a flexible configuration with a hybrid network to connect to other cloud or local networks.

Default or dedicated location. This refers to the hardware configuration. The default settings allow one decision per resource. Dedicated locks any resources created in that VPC to be on dedicated hardware at an additional cost.

Custom VPC facts
Private IP and public IPv4

Assignment of 1 mandatory private IPv4 CIDR blocks

- Prefix min /28 (16 IP)
- Max /16 prefix (65,536 IP)

Can add secondary IPv4 blocks after creation.

- A maximum of 5 can be increased with a support ticket.
- When you think of VPC, you have a pool of private IPv4 addresses and you can use public addresses when needed.

Single Assigned CIDR IPv6 /56 block

- Even in the maturing phase, not everything works the same way as IPv4.
- With the increasing use of IPv6, this should be added as default.
- AWS assigns the range since you have no choice about which range to use, or you can choose to use your own IPv6 addresses.
- IPv6 doesn't have private addresses; they are all addressed as public by default.

DNS provided by R53

Available at the base IP address of VPC + 2. If the VPC is 10.0.0.0, the DNS IP will be 10.0.0.2. Two options that manage how the DNS works in the VPC:

- Edit DNS hostnames
- If true, public DNS hostnames are assigned to instances with public IPs in a VPC.
- If false, this is not available.
- Edit DNS resolution
- If true, the instances in the VPC can use the DNS IP address.
- If false, this is not available.

VPC subnets

AZ Strong VPC subnet.

- If the Available zone fails, the subnet and services also fail.
- High availability requires multiple components in different AZs.
- One subnet can only have 1 AZ.

- 1 AZ can have zero or more subnets.
- CIDR IPv4 is a subset of the VID CIDR block.
- Impossible to overlap with other subnets in that VPC
- Optionally, the IPv6 CIDR block can be assigned to the subnet.
- (256/64 subnets can be adapted to /56 VPC)
- Subnets can interact with other subnets in the VPC by default.

Reserved IP addresses

There are five IP addresses within each VPC subnet that cannot be used. Whatever the size of the subnet, there are five fewer IP addresses than you expect.

DHCP Option Set

This is how IT devices automatically receive IP addresses. There are several options applied simultaneously to a VPC and this configuration flows through the subnets. This can be changed, new ones can be created, but one cannot be changed. If you want to change the settings:

You can create a new one

- Change VPC mapping to new
- Delete the old

IP allocation options

Automatically assign public IPv4 address

- This creates a public IP address in addition to your private subnet.
- This is necessary to make a subnet public.
- Automatically assigns IPv6 address.
- For this to work, the subnet and the VPC need an address assignment.

VPC Routing and Internet Gateway

VPC Router is a high availability device available in every VPC that moves traffic from one place to another. The router has a network interface on each subnet of the VPC. Route traffic between subnets. Routing tables define what the VPC router will do with the traffic when the data leaves that subnet. A VPC is created with a primary route table. If a custom route table is not associated with a subnet, it uses the main route table of the VPC.

If you associate a custom route table created with a subnet, the main route table is decoupled. A subnet can only have one routing table at a time, but a routing table can be associated with many subnets.

Route tables

When traffic leaves the subnet with which this routing table is associated, the VPC router examines the IP packets for the destination address. Traffic will try to match the route to the routing table. If multiple routes are found as a match, the prefix is then used as a priority. The higher the prefix, the more definite the route will be, therefore, the higher the priority. If the destination indicates local, it means that the destination is in the VPC itself. The local route can never be updated, they are always present, and the local route always takes precedence. This is the objection to the prefix rule.

Internet portal

A managed service that permits gateway traffic between the Internet and the VPC or the AWS public area (S3, SQS, SNS, etc.). Regional resilient gateway connected to a VPC. An IGW will cover all AZs in a region used by the VPC. A VPC can have:

- An IGW
- No IGW and be completely private.

IGW can be created and connected to any VPC. It works within the AWS public area.

Using IGW

In this example, an EC2 instance has:

- Private IP address from 10.16.16.20
- Public address of 43,250.192.20

The public address is not public and is linked to the EC2 instance itself. Instead, IGW creates a record that links the instance's private IP to the public IP. That is why the private IP address is only displayed when creating an EC2 instance. This is important. For IPv4, it's not configured in the operating system with the public address.

Summary

The Virtual Private Cloud administration gives the systems administration establishment to EC2 and different AWS administrations. AWS abstracts some systems administration segments so that their arrangement is simpler than in a customary system; however, despite everything, you have to have a strong handle of systems administration basics to engineer VPCs.

In every area, AWS consequently furnishes a default VPC with default subnets, a primary course table, a default security gathering, and a default NACL. Many utilize a default VPC for quite a while, never arranging a VPC without any preparation. This makes it even more significant that you, as an AWS engineer, see how to arrange a virtual system foundation without any preparation. There's a decent possibility you won't be permitted to adjust a framework that was based over a default VPC. Rather, you might be entrusted with duplicating it starting from the earliest stage—investigating different issues en route. Practice what you've realized in this section until making completely useful VPCs turns out to be natural to you.

In a conventional system, you're allowed to reconfigure server IP addresses, move them to various subnets, and even move them to various physical areas. You have huge adaptability to change your arrangements midstream.

Exercise
Allocate and use an elastic IP Address

1. Allocate an elastic IP address and associate it with the instance you created earlier.
2. Click Allocate New Address.
3. Click Allocate.
4. Click the EIP, and under the Actions menu, click Associate Address.

5. Select the instance you created earlier.
6. Click Associate. The instance original public IP address should change to the EIP.

AWS CERTIFICATION EXAM
IN FIVE STEPS

I am addicted to certification! I have been receiving IT certifications for over 18 years, have passed 50+ exams during this period, and have failed only twice for one exam.

I will explain how to pass the AWS certification exams the first time.

The key to passing the AWS certification exams is simply preparing properly. Preparation includes the following five steps that I will explain in this post:

- Practice (practice)
- Training (mainly online video)
- Theory (read)
- Practical questions
- Take the test

BACKGROUND OF THE INVESTIGATION

Many people who take these exams have basic computer skills. It may be much more difficult for you if you are a newcomer and cannot distinguish a block from an object store or container virtual machine. That said, you don't need to have great skills in the underlying technologies that support AWS since cloud computing removes much of that complexity.

Many developers unfamiliar with the infrastructure get along well with AWS because it provides them with the gears they need to get the job done without worrying about how the underlying layers work.

In the exam plan, AWS makes the following recommendations for AWS-specific knowledge and experience. The good news is that all of this knowledge can be gained through hands-on experience and free article reading on the AWS website.

The exam recently changed the format this year and the following image shows the variances between the earlier and the latter format (this applies to all AWS certification exams at the corresponding level).

AWS technology is evolving incredibly fast, so I would recommend using the recent exam format if you start your studies now as it will better match the features available today. It is not as generous as the greater difficulty of some of the questions on the new exam. But don't be discouraged, the accompanying exams aren't too difficult, and you have plenty of resources to prepare.

STEP 1: IT ALL BEGINS WITH PRACTICE

One of the keys to learning technology is to play with it. Don't worry if you don't work with AWS. Not everybody has the chance to work with the technologies they study in a professional context, and surely, I have passed many exams without real work experience.

AWS allows you to create an account for free, and the free tier allows you to use specific AWS services for free. Go to:

https://aws.amazon.com/free.

The free tier offers many free services every month, including (among others):

Free AWS tier: It's a great way to gain experience, and you can take things out and take them apart without costing you a penny. It's amazing what you can do on the free tier for a whole year!

STEP 2: ONLINE VIDEO TRAINING

Online video training is an excellent tool. There are many AWS certification courses online that allow you to relax and absorb everything. The best fact about the video is that it has an experienced instructor who can guide you through technology and give you useful tips to pass the exam.

Classes can range from PowerPoint to highly lab-oriented, and this is where the problem of their isolated use lies. Courses with a lot of content can be very dry and boring, and more practical courses will be light and will help you get ready to take the exam.

To make sure you pass the exam and gain hands-on experience on AWS for the first time, sign up for the latest AWS Certified cloud practioner hands-on video training in digital cloud training.

STEP 3: THEORY

Some people find it boring, but there is no substitute for theory, and there is still plenty to read. I like to practice a lot of IT before I get caught up in the theoretical part that really helps things make sense (and keeps it interesting). It is essential to keep practicing as you gain more knowledge: use it or lose it!

The AWS website contains a wealth of information, so you can use it pretty much if you want. There are books and e-books, too, but things are changing rapidly in the AWS world and are generally updated with time.

My strategy in learning theory is to take lots of notes. When I look at the online courses, I also pay attention to the most essential facts. Having concise and summary training notes becomes invaluable when you try to remember thousands of facts because you can come back to them at any time without having to read long articles. Try a digital note-taking tool like Microsoft OneNote or Evernote.

STEP 4: PRACTICAL QUESTION

One of the most important tools to learn and assess whether you are ready for the exam is practice questions. Using high-quality, practical questions will help you understand the types of questions you may encounter during the exam and help you identify weaknesses.

However, the challenge is to find good quality practice questions. There have always been many exams on the Internet, and various companies have low-quality questions (which they generally copy between themselves).

I suggest that you test multiple times during your preparation, don't wait for the exam time to come. The practical questions should be considered both a learning tool and an assessment tool, and therefore should be used from the beginning.

STEP 5: EXAM TIME

Another key to my success in IT certification exams is that I have never booked the exam before, I am sure I am ready. You should receive 80 to 90% of the practical questions just before you think about booking. The actual pass rate is much lower than this, but there will always be surprises during the day with technologies you haven't covered enough during training.

Once you've trained, taken a course, viewed my training notes, and passed the training questions, you're ready to go. If you prepared well, you don't have to get crowded at the last minute, so get rid of all the stress and come back.

Try to read each question first and see the answers. You can develop talent for this and often quickly discover what the answer will be. Go back to the question in detail and make sure you haven't forgotten anything before choosing.

Some questions are an objective, a multiple choice with multiple answers, and you may need to select "all that apply." Make sure you are not mistaken, as it is an easy mistake to make!

If you're stuck with a question, give the best answer and bookmark it for review and come back at the end. It's a good way to make sure you don't get too stressed out and hope you have enough time, in the end, to think about it more. Just check the answers for which you really need the most time.

AWS certification exams are fairly well written, so there are generally not many confusing questions. If you have prepared high-quality, practical questions to prepare yourself, you will need to be well equipped to handle everything. Good study and good luck with your exams!

AMAZON AURORA

Aurora's architecture is VERY different from RDS. It uses a cluster that is a single primary instance or zero or more replicas. Replicas within Aurora can be used for readings during normal operation. It provides the benefits of multi-AZ RDS and read replicas. Aurora does not use local storage for compute instances. An Aurora cluster possesses a shared cluster volume. It provides faster provisioning, improved availability, and best performance. The Aurora cluster works in different Availability Zones.

There are one main instance and multiple replicas. Applications read by applications can use replicas. There is a shared memory of up to 64 TiBs in all replicas. This uses six copies throughout AZ. All instances can access these storage nodes. This replication occurs at the file level. No additional resources are consumed during replication.

By default, the main instance is the only one that can write. The replicas will have read access. Aurora automatically detects hardware failures in shared memory. If an error occurs, immediately repair that area of the disk and recreate the data without damage. With Aurora, you can acquire up to 15 replicas, and each can be a failover destination. Failover will be faster because no memory changes are necessary.

- The shared cluster volume is based on SSD storage by default.
- It provides such high IOPS and low latency.
- There is no way to select magnetic storage.
- This is based on what is consumed.
- Billing with a high score or billed by the most used.
- The released memory can be reused.

If you reduce a large amount of storage space, you will need to create a new cluster and migrate the data from the old cluster to the new cluster. Storage is for the cluster and not for the instances, which means you can add and remove replicas without archiving, provisioning, or deleting.

Aurora endpoint

- Minimum endpoints
- The cluster endpoint always points to the main instance.
- This is used to read and write applications.

Reader endpoint

- It will point to the main instance if that's all there is.
- It will load the balance between all replicas available for read operations.
- The additional replicas used for the readings will automatically balance based on the load.

Costs

- No free level option
- Aurora does not support micro instances
- Beyond RDS single AZ (micro), Aurora offers the best value.
- The calculation is billed per second with a minimum of 10 minutes.
- The file is billed with a lifetime watermark with GB-Month.
- Additional I/O cost per request made to the cluster shared storage.

- 100% DB size in backups is included for free.
- The 100GB cluster will have 100GB of backup space.

Aurora Restore, Clone and Backtrack

Backups in Aurora work the same way as RDS. Restorations create a new cluster. The backtrack must be cluster enabled. This allows you to restore the database to an earlier time. This helps to corrupt the data. You can adjust the backspace of the window for which it will work.

Quick clones make a new database much faster than copying all the data. It refers to the original memory and writes only the differences between the two. It uses a small amount of memory and only stores data that has been changed in the clone or the original after cloning.

Aurora serverless

Provides a version of the Aurora database product without managing resources. It still creates a cluster but uses ACU or Aurora Capacity Unit. For a cluster, a minimum and maximum ACU can be set based on the load and can even drop to 0 to pause.

- Billing is based on resources used per second.
- The same resistance of Aurora (6 copies in AZ).

ACUs are stateless and shared among many AWS clients and have no local storage. They can be quickly assigned to the serverless Aurora cluster when needed. Once ACUs have been assigned to a cluster, they have access to the cluster storage in the same way as a provisioned Aurora cluster.

There is a shared proxy fleet. When a client interacts with the data, it is actually communicating with the proxy fleet. The proxy fleet streams an app with the ACU and ensures it can scale in and out without worrying about usage. AWS manages it on your behalf.

Aurora Serverless - Use Cases

- Rarely used applications.
- Low volume blog site.
- Pay only for resources while consuming per second.
- New applications with unpredictable workloads.
- Excellent for variable workloads like sales cycles. Can be expanded and reduced according to demand
- Good for database development and testing, you can resize it when not needed.
- Excellent for multi-tenant applications.
- Bill a user a dollar amount per month per license.
- If the incoming load is directly connected to multiple inputs, this makes sense.

Aurora Global Database

Presents the idea of secondary regions with up to 16 read-only replicas.

- Excellent for cross-region disaster recovery and business continuity.
- Global reading scale
- Low latency performance improvements for international customers.
- The application can perform read operations against read replicas.
- There are ~ 1s or less replication between regions.
- It is a one-way replica.
- No additional CPU usage is required; this happens at the storage level.
- Secondary regions can have 16 replicas.
- Everything can be promoted to read or write in a DR situation.
- Maximum 5 secondary regions.

Aurora Multi-Master writes

This allows a cluster of auroras to have multiple instances that can read and write.

- Single master mode
- one R/W and zero or more read-only replicas
- The cluster endpoint is normally used to write
- The read endpoint is used to balance the load.

Aurora Multi-master does not have an endpoint or load balancer. An application can connect to one or both instances within a multi-master cluster. When one of the R/W nodes gets a written request from the application, it instantly proposes that the data be committed to all file notes in that cluster. At this point, each node that forms a cluster confirms or rejects the proposed change. It will be denied if this conflicts with something that is already in flight.

The write instance searches for a group of nodes to be agreed upon. If the group rejects it, it mistakenly cancels the write. Otherwise, it will replicate to all storage nodes in the cluster. This also ensures that the storage space is refreshed in the cache memory of other nodes. If a writer falls into a multi-master cluster, the application will move all future load to a new writer with little or no interruption.

DMS - Database migration service

A managed database migration service. It starts with a replication instance running on an EC2 instance. This replication instance performs one or more replication tasks. This is where the settings for database migration are defined. This is done using a replication instance. The origin and destination endpoints must be defined. These point to the physical and target databases. One of these endpoints must be on AWS.

Full load migration is a unique process that transfers everything at once. This requires that the database be inactive during this process. This could take several days. Instead, Full Load + CDC allows you to perform a full load transfer and monitors any changes that occur during this period. Any changes acquired can be applied to the target. CDC migration is only valid if you have a provider solution that only changes need to be captured and works quickly. The SCT (Schema Conversion Tool) can perform conversions between types of databases.

HOW TO UNDERSTAND THE
AWS ENVIRONMENT

Understanding of the AWS environment is necessary for the proper utilization of cloud resources on the platform. It is a veritable tool for beginners and professional architects to learn how to run web and application servers in the cloud for hosting websites and other online activities.

Amazon Web Services is a secure cloud environment that provides database storage; compute power, content delivery, together with other features for business growth and development.

Features Of AWS Cloud Platform

Here are some notable features of AWS cloud services:

- It helps in sending bulk e-mails to your customers.
- AWS is important for using managed databases like MySQL, Oracle, PostgreSQL, and SQL servers for storing data in the cloud.
- Used for hosting active websites by running web and application servers in the cloud.
- Relevant for storing all your files and contents on the cloud in a way that you can access them using different devices.
- Valuable for global delivery of your contents and files quickly through CDN – Content Delivery Network.

Overview Of Common Terminologies Used On The Platform

Some common terminologies associated with Amazon Web Services.

1. Edge location – these are endpoints for Content Delivery Network –CDN used for CloudFront.
2. Region – a geographical location with one or more availability zones.
3. Availability Zone – a data center on Amazon AWS.

AWS Infrastructure For Global Services

This is the most secure, reliable, and extensive cloud platform providing numerous fully-featured services from data centers worldwide. It helps deploy application workloads across the globe using a single click and offers the capacity and technology for developing and deploying specific applications useful for your end-users in seconds. This is the best cloud infrastructure available for architectural designs globally.

Millions of active users operate the platform, and it features the largest and engaging ecosystem. Their customers range from start-ups, enterprises, and public sector agencies that are operating at least a use case.

AWS has a well-organized structure with various features and categories such as

- Seventy-seven availability zones.
- Twenty-four launched regions.
- Three announced regions.
- One local zone with two-wavelength zones.
- 2 Two times more regions.
- It serves two hundred and forty-five countries and territories.
- Two hundred and sixteen points of presence, including two hundred and five edge locations and eleven edge caches.
- Ninety-seven direct connect locations.

Hosting cloud-based infrastructure and realizing greater performance, security, and scale anywhere is the reason most customers are opting for Amazon Web Services. In the Magic Quadrant for Cloud Organization as a Service, Worldwide developed by Garner, AWS is seen as the leader for the 9th time in a row. It has the highest score in both axes of measurement. That means the ability to execute and complete vision and ranking as one of the top six vendors in the business.

The Benefits Of AWS Infrastructure For Global Services

1. Scalability of the cloud – users take advantage of the infinite ideological scalability of the cloud. They enjoy over provision with enough capacity for handling business operations during peak level of activity. This step will reduce expenditures and position the customer to meet their needs. Organizations can mop up resources quickly as occasion demands and deploy numerous servers without hassles.

2. Security – AWS core infrastructure is designed to measure up to the most stringent security requirements globally. This infrastructure is monitored 24 hours of the day to maintain confidentiality, integrity, and data availability. This helps to ensure automatic data encryption at the physical level before such data goes into circulation. That means all the data used in the AWS global network, which interconnects regions and data centers, are encrypted automatically. Building on your infrastructure is possible since you can manage your data, encrypt, and transfer it whenever you want.

3. Global Footprint – AWS global footprint is always enlarging at a greater proportion, and it is the largest infrastructure footprint among other providers. It would help if you chose a technology infrastructure when deploying your workloads and applications to the cloud. Ensure that your chosen technology is closer to the end-users. It is advisable to run your workloads on the cloud of a vendor that supports a wide range of applications, including those

having the lowest latency needs and highest throughput. But if your data is in the clouds, apply AWS Ground Station that can provide satellite antennas closer to the regions with AWS infrastructure.

4. Availability – when you talk of network availability, AWS can provide the highest network availability amongst other cloud providers. You are bound to experience fewer downtime hours. Every region is separated and consists of several businesses, which are part and parcel of AWS infrastructure. You can enjoy a higher availability of data by isolating issues and partitioning applications across numerous vendors in the region. Moreover, the management console and control planes of Amazon Web Services are fully distributed across the regions, including regional API endpoints. These are built to operate securely for twenty-four hours if isolated from the global control plane functionalities. Therefore, customers are not required to access the region or its API endpoints through external networks during periods of isolation.

5. Performance – the infrastructure of Amazon Web Services are designed for high performance. The regions produce low latency, low packet loss with a high overall network quality. A fully redundant 100 Gibe fiber network backbone helps in achieving this feature. Most times, this provides various terabits of capacity between regions. Telco providers with AWS Wavelength and Local Zones offer greater performance for applications that need single-digit millisecond latencies. This helps deliver AWS infrastructure and services closer to the customers, who are end-users 5G connected devices. No matter the needs of your applications, you can gather relevant resources by deploying numerous servers in a few minutes.

6. Flexibility – AWS global infrastructure offers you the flexibility of deciding how and where you want to operate your workloads. If you carry cut this operation, you are using the same control plane,

AWS services, APIs, and network as the case may be. Running your applications globally will require you to select from any of the AWS regions, including the AZs. Choose AWS wavelength or AWS Local Zones if you need to run your applications with single-digit millisecond latencies to mobile devices and customers. You can choose AWS Outposts if you decide to run your programs on-premises.

Global Infrastructure For AWS By Regions

AS I said earlier, the AWS global infrastructure is the most reliable, secure, and extensive cloud platform with over one hundred and seventy-five fully-featured services coming from global data centers. You can deploy your workloads and applications across the globe in a single click. Amazon Web Services offers you a reliable cloud infrastructure whenever you desire it. Therefore, you can also design or create specific applications nearer to your end-users with a single-digit millisecond latency.

Here is a statistics of AWS Global Infrasture according to regions:

S/N	Regions	Number of Availability Zones
1.	US East (North Virginia)	6
2.	US East (Ohio)	3
3.	US West (North California)	3
4.	US West (Oregon)	4
5.	Asia Pacific (Mumbai)	3
6.	Asia Pacific (Seoul)	4
7.	Asia Pacific (Singapore)	3

8.	Asia Pacific (Sydney)	3
9.	Asia Pacific (Tokyo)	4
10.	Asia Pacific (Osaka Local)	1
11.	Asia Pacific (Hong Kong SAR)	3
12.	Canada Central	2
13.	Mainland China (Beijing)	2
14.	Mainland China (Ningxia)	3
15.	Europe (Frankfurt)	3
16.	Europe (Ireland)	3
17.	Europe (London)	3
18.	Europe (Milan)	3
19.	Europe (Paris)	3
20.	Europe (Stockholm)	3
21.	South America (Sao Paulo)	3
22.	GovCloud (US) US-East	3
23.	GovCloud (US) US-West	3
24.	Middle East (Bahrain)	3
25.	Africa (Cape Town)	3

Global Infrastructure For AWS By Zones

Over a million customers in more than one hundred and ninety countries benefit from the services of Amazon Web Services. AWS aims to achieve higher throughput and lower latency through expansion and ensuring that their data remains only in the specified region. This is possible through the provision of infrastructure that meets their global requirements.

The cloud infrastructure of AWS is designed around AWS regions and Availability zones. These regions are physical locations in the world with numerous availability zones. These zones are made of one or more data centers having redundant power, connectivity, networking, and housed in different facilities.

These zones enable you to run production applications with databases that are scalable, highly available, and fault-tolerant than what obtains in a single data center. Amazon web services operate in more than sixty Availability zones in over twenty geographical regions globally. There are also announced plans for more availability zones and regions.

AWS regions are independent of other AWS regions. This helps them to maintain stability with fault tolerance features. Every availability zone is independent, but they are connected using low-latency links throughout a region. It offers you the flexibility of placing instances and storing data in multiple geographic regions, including numerous availability zones within a specific region.

Every availability zone is built as a separate failure zone. Therefore availability zones are isolated physically within a typical metropolitan region and situated in lower-risk flood plains. Different flood zones categorization is not the same throughout AWS regions.

These zones feature an uninterruptible power supply (UPS) system and onsite backup generation facilities with data centers based in various availability zones. They are made to be supplied by independent substations and minimize the danger of an event on the power grid affecting more than a single availability zone. All availability zones are connected redundantly to several tier-1 transit providers.

Global Infrastructure For AWS By Edge Locations

Global infrastructure is a region where AWS is based around the world. It is a set of high-level IT services, including regions, availability zones, edge locations, and regional edge caches.

Edge locations are known as points of presence and include sites deployed globally in major cities and areas with many populations. AWS services like Lambda@Edge, including AWS CloudFront, use edge locations for caching data and reducing latency for end-user access. A customer could be in Seattle, and the data is stored in Singapore; CloudFront identifies the original place of the request and moves data from Singapore to an edge location nearer to the customer.

Therefore another request from Seattle can access the data faster than the former request since the system can access the data the Edge storage in Seattle. Therefore, it does not have to go back to Singapore and reduces latency through that process.

Regional edge caches help to improve performance because they have greater cache-width than individual edge location. This makes your objects to remain in cache longer at these locations. It keeps more of your content nearer to the viewers, thereby minimizing the need for CloudFront to return to the original web server. This also helps to enhance the general performance of the system for viewers.

AWS customers enjoy an efficient process of architecting and deploying infrastructure, application, and service on a platform that is resilient, scalable, fault-tolerant, and highly available. This exceptional service could be achieved by launching multiple EC22 instances in various availability zones.

AMAZON ELASTIC CONTAINER SERVICE (ECS)

Virtualization issues

Using the EC2 virtual machine with Nitro Hypervisor, 4 GB of RAM, and 40 GB of disk, the operating system can consume 60 to 70% of the disk and most of the available memory. Containers take advantage of the similarities of multiple guests' operating systems by eliminating duplicate resources. This allows applications to run in their isolated environments.

Image anatomy

A Docker image consists of multiple layers and not a monolithic disk image. Each row of a Docker image creates a new file system level on top of the previous one. Images are created from scratch or a basic image. Images contain read-only layers, and images are layered in images.

The Docker container is the same as the Docker image, except it has an additional READ/WRITE level of the container. If you have many containers with very similar basic structures, they will share the overlapping parts. The other layers we are reused between the containers.

Container registration

Registration or container image center. Dockerfile can create an image of the container where it is stored in the container registry. The Docker hosts can also run several containers based on one or more images. A single image can spawn containers on many different Docker hosts.

Key concepts of the container:

- Docker files are used in creating Docker images.
- The containers are portable and always work as expected.
- As long as there is a compatible host, it will run exactly as expected.
- Containers are lightweight, use the host operating system to lift heavy loads.
- File system levels are shared whenever possible.
- Containers run only the application and environment required for execution.
- The ports must be exposed to allow external access from the host and beyond.
- Application stacks can be multiple containers.

ECS - Container Service concepts:

- Accept the containers and instructions provided.
- ECS allows you to create a cluster (the cluster is where the containers come from).
- Container images will be found in a log.
- AWS provides ECR (Elastic Container Record)
- Dockerhub can also be used.

The container definition provides ECS with sufficient information about the individual container. Task definitions store resources used by the activity. This stores the task role, which is an IAM role that allows the task to access other AWS resources. However, the task itself is not highly available. So, the ECS service is configured by defining the service and represents the number of copies of a task that you want to scale and HA.

ECS Cluster Types

The ECS cluster manages:

- Planning and orchestration

- Cluster management
- Positioning motor

EC2 mode

The ECS cluster is created in a VPC. You benefit from the multiple AZs found within that VPC. You specify an initial size that will guide an automatic resizing group. ECS using EC2 mode isn't a serverless solution, so you need to worry about cluster capacity. The Container instances aren't delivered as a managed service; they are managed as normal EC2 instances. You can use spot prices or EC2 prepaid servers.

Fargate mode

This eliminates a significant portion of ECS administration overhead, which means no need to administer EC2. Fargate's shared infrastructure allows all clients to access the same pool of resources. The Fargate distribution still uses a cluster with a VPC in which AZs are specified. For ECS activities, they are injected into the VPC. Each activity is assigned an elastic network interface with an IP address within the VPC. They are then run as a VPC resource, and you pay only for the resources of the container you use.

EC2 vs. ECS (EC2) vs. Fargate

- If you are already using containers, use ECS.
- EC2 mode is useful for a high workload when the price is taken into account. This allows for spot and prepaid prices.
- Fargate is fantastic if you
- has a heavy workload but is aware of the overall costs.
- Have small or explosive style workloads.
- Use periodic or batch workloads.

AWS CERTIFICATION EXAM TIPS

We now have what I term as a "limitless access" to information. When I started with IT years back, I relied mainly on books, which is obviously one of the best ways to prepare for your AWS exams. Back then, free information on the Internet was much more limited, and if you wanted to build a home lab, you would end up spending thousands of dollars-worth on equipment and spend a spare on it!

A lot has changed and for those of us looking for AWS certifications, today have implausible options. You can find quality, inexpensive courses you need to help you pass the exam. You can also get free courses online. And to top it off, you can train for free with a free AWS tier account.

So perhaps the question you should be asking is, why is no one passing their exams? The reality is that all required materials are available regardless of your budget, but it is up to us to use them correctly. So how can you make sure you don't pass the AWS certification exam? Here are some tips:

Tip #1: Own your accomplishments

This can apply to almost anything in life. This is one of the first things that experts in any discipline will highlight. This simply tells that it is your responsibility to gather all the necessary information, take the time to learn it, and effort to make sure you are ready for your AWS exam. If you're wrong, own it, find out what it is that you did wrong and fix it.

Tip #2: Be an active student

We can sit on the couch, watch videos, and take in as many facts as possible without even thinking. But to keep the information, you must actively participate. This means actively taking notes, solving problems, taking practical exercises, and doing practice tests. The more you know the practice, the better. Answering questions from other students in forums is a very good exercise that requires only a little research.

Tip #3: Know your weaknesses

Taking on practical tests will give you information on your area of weakness. Be sure to use the information and also study these areas in more detail. For instance, if you're still confused by questions about Instances vs. Amazon EBS, go back to your training, notes, or watch the videos again. You can also search both services on google or the AWS website for the use cases related to each service, then go ahead and take exercises on your free tier account.

Tip #4: Take the time to exercise regularly

Trying to learn Sporadically will be is your enemy because you tend to these forgets things faster. It is better to fix a specific study period every day and stick to it until the end. Try rescheduling the timing to when your brain is fresh and full of energy. For me, it means early morning.

Tip #5: Use the practice tests in advance

Some people wait up to a week or two passes to start using the practice tests. Today there are a lot of practice test providers out there that ask questions very similar to the actual exam. Register and start taking the exams. It doesn't matter if you fail miserably at first, the fact is that you will get to learn the style of the questions and gain more insight. Be sure to follow each test and record your weaknesses so you can work on it.

Tip #6: Find cool projects

If you're taking a course with hands-on lab exercises, it's great but tries creating your projects too. If you follow a script, you learn less. When you create your projects, you learn much more because you have to correct your mistakes. If you don't know AWS, start with a hands-on lab lesson to learn the basics, then suggest your projects or variations.

Tip #7: Don't book your exam until you're ready

Sometimes employers expect their employees to obtain a certificate within a reasonable time. If possible, postpone the exam until you are sure you can easily pass it. For AWS certification students, I always recommend consistently passing 80-90% before booking exams. But remember, this may lead to a false sense of confidence when you exercise again from time to time.

These are just a few tips that can help you. Everyone has their own learning style, and this may be a preference for reading, video, or hands-on activities. Design your training to fit perfectly into your learning style, but don't overlook others, as ALL are required to pass the exams.

AMAZON BLOCK AND FILE STORAGE

A WS service storage is a service that allows you to store data by moving it over the Internet or another network to an offsite storage system managed by a third party, from personal storage for hosting or backing up someone's private mail, images, videos, and other private files, to professional storage that businesses use as a backup solution. The distance where they can securely transfer, store, and share data files.

AWS service storage is an attractive cloud storage solution offered by Amazon to service providers to meet modern data storage scenarios. With an AWS service AWS storage account, you can access two types of storage services:

Storage systems are generally expandable to suit the data storage needs of each individual or organization, accessible from any location, and versatile to allow any type of device to access it. There are three main models for businesses to choose from: a public cloud storage service:

- Consolidate the storage infrastructure

The solution combines the better of two approaches with physical arrays for data center deployments and virtual arrays for smaller enterprise surroundings, such as remote sites or branch offices that require NAS (Network Attached Storage) storage.

- Automate data management

- Manage your data growth more efficiently.
- Improve IT agility and boost your business
- Accelerate business intelligence and decision-making with fast and innovative data movement between remote sites/subsidiaries/data centers and the cloud The solution allows you to save administration hours and reduce costs by up to 60%.
- Are there any hidden costs in AWS service storage?

No, there are no hidden fees related to AWS service storage. However, in order to properly calculate the storage costs for your specific application.

The Scale of AWS service storage?

In terms of the scale required to bring applications closer to users around the world, Amazon covers more areas of the world than any other cloud provider.

AWS service storage Data Redundancy

Data redundancy and storage replication are very well supported in Amazon AWS to ensure that data is stored permanently and does not get lost. AWS service storage replication backs up data across multiple sites to protect it from any (natural) disaster, power outage, hardware failure, or any other planned or unplanned event. The four types of Amazon data redundancy are:

- Redundant local storage (LRS): the data is copied in triplicate in the same data center.
- Redundant storage by zone (ZRS): the data is replicated synchronously on three storage clusters in the same region.

Being an excellent cloud service as it is, AWS service storage is constantly updated, extended and innovated by the Amazon team. Recently, at Ignite, new products are to be presented, and are briefly mentioned here because of their relevance for service providers.

AWS service storage types.

- Amazon blob Storage:
- Table Storage
- Queue Storage
- Disk Storage
- File Storage

Amazon offers a storage service within its cloud AWS offer. AWS service storage works on the principle of amazon blob (binary large object), data structures in which one can place any type of binary or text data. Amazon offers the storage of three types of amazon blob, depending on whether it is a block of data for large volumes of data...

Three redundancy levels are offered with a lbs. mode (locally redundant storage) with data replication restricted to a single geographic region, a grs mode (geographically redundant storage) with geographic replication between two distant geographic regions, and finally a ra- mode. Grs.

The amazon StorSimple option is a hybrid storage offer that combines cloud storage in AWS with a storage array located on company premises. This solution is accessible to amazon AWS customers whose annual bill exceeds 40 k € (approximately 62.5 TB of data hosted in AWS). In this case, amazon installs a xyratex 7020 storage array in the enterprise. This accelerates access to data stored locally but relies on AWS to extend the capacities of the bay thanks to the cloud. You can thus set up a geo-replication of local data to Amazon AWS data centers in Dublin or Amsterdam.

AWS service storage: capacity three types of storage offered: amazon blob objects of block type, amazon blob objects of page and disc type, and finally, tables and queues. A file mode is in preview.

Access management windows AWS active directory allows you to extend the company's active directory to AWS cloud services.

Interfaces the availability of a rest API to access storage services.

Hd insight (Hadoop cluster implementation) and StorSimple (hybrid hosting with a storage bay placed in the company and connected to AWS) options.

Sla 99.99% guaranteed data access.

Data location 15 datacenters in 5 global geographic regions to choose from: united states, Europe (Dublin and Amsterdam), Asia / pacific, japan, brazil.

Amazon blob in page mode (€ 0.038 per GB per month the first tb in lrs mode, € 0.071 in grs mode and € 0.09 in ra-grs mode), tables and queues (€ 0.053 per gb and per month the first tb in lrs mode, € 0.071 in grs mode and 0, € 09 in ra-grs mode).

More keynotes on types of AWS storage account

AWS service storage offers several types of AWS storage accounts.

The types of AWS storage accounts offered are:

block amazon blob AWS storage accounts: amazon blob object AWS storage accounts only with premium performance characteristics.

File AWS storage accounts: recommended for business or high-performance scaling applications.

Amazon blob AWS storage accounts: old amazon blob AWS storage accounts only.

Cloud storage is an extremely valuable service today: it is inexpensive, saves a huge amount of capacity on computers and in data centers, and saves you from having to add additional storage to your system. Amazon offers storage solutions for individuals and businesses, ranging from 5 GB of free cloud storage to 1 TB of cloud storage on one drive with an office365 (o365) account and almost infinitely scalable storage solutions

- Know more about the following and their importance.
- AWS blobs: massively scalable object memory for text and binary data.
- AWS queues: a messaging memory for reliable messaging between application components.
- AWS tables: nosql memory for storage without structured data schema.

An intro to AWS cloud shell

AWS cloud shell is a free bash shell, which you can run directly in the AWS portal. The AWS CLI interface is preinstalled and configured for use with your account. Click the cloud shell menu button located in the upper right corner of the AWS portal window:

You can also install and use AWS CLI locally.

An AWS service AWS storage account contains all of your AWS service storage data objects: amazon blob, files, queues, tables, and disks. The data in your AWS service AWS storage account is durable and highly available, secure and massively scalable.

The AWS free account.

The AWS free account, like its name, is totally free, and you also get a credit of € 170 that you can use within 30 days. Once you've exhausted your free credit, you will be notified.

AWS service storage amazon blob stores large amounts of unstructured object data, such as text or binary data. Amazon blob AWS service storage is highly scalable and available. Customers can access data objects in amazon blob storage with power shell or AWS CLI, programmatically through AWS service storage client libraries.

The amazon blob storage offers three types of resources which are:

- the AWS storage account.
- a container in the AWS storage account.
- An amazon blob in a container.

The AWS service storage service supports three types of amazon blob:

- The block amazon blob stores only text and binary data, up to about 4.7 tb...
- Add amazon blobs consist of blocks, like block amazon blobs, but are optimized for add operations. Addition, amazon blobs are great for scenarios such as logging data from virtual machines.
- Page amazon blob objects store random access files up to 8 TB in size. Page amazon blob objects store virtual hard disk files and serve as disks for AWS virtual machines.

Move data to amazon blob storage; several solutions exist to migrate existing data to amazon blob storage: azcopy is an easy-to-use command-line tool for windows and Linux that copies data to and from amazon blob storage, between containers or between AWS storage accounts. AWS data factory supports copying data to and from amazon blob storage with an account key, shared access signature, service principal, or managed identities for AWS resources.

Amazon blobfuse is a virtual file system driver for amazon blob AWS service storage. You can use amazon blobfuse to access your existing block amazon blob data in your AWS storage account via the Linux file system.

Object Storage vs Block Storage

In traditional IT environments, there are two types of storage, block storage, and file storage. These types exist with different providers such as AWS, open stack, and oracle.

Block Storage operates the data at a low level, at a raw storage level, and manages the data as a group of numbered blocks.

File Storage operates at a higher level, at the operating system level, and handles data as a hierarchy of files and directories. This type of storage is intimately related to the one used by the operating system.

S3 object storage is a bit different. The storage is independent of a server is accessed through the internet. The data is managed by an API (Application Program Interface) over HTTP.

Each object contains data and metadata. They are contained in buckets and have a key (filename) associated. Buckets are directories on which no more directories can be built and can contain an unlimited number of objects (files).

It is impossible to lie a bucket, open an object, install an operating system within S3, or run a database.

S3 is automatically replicated through multiple devices in multiple facilities within a region.

Similarly, the scalability, if the requests grow constantly, Amazon S3 will automatically partition the buckets to support many simultaneous requests.

If traditional storage is required, AWS provides EBS, used by EC2. Also, EFS (Elastic File System) that provides storage that can be associated with multiple instances of EC2.

CONCLUSION

T hank you for reaching the end. Finally, we give you some tips from the cloud community that we hope you have an idea for this test. This book will equip you with a good sense of AWS performance, best security practices, underwriting, and compliance storage capabilities.

Therefore, you need to understand more about the basics of the service to pass exams. You should also be familiar with scenarios in which a particular service may be used. Therefore, you should consider these architectures and try to understand them as much as possible.

Based on the facts above, we can conclude that there is a huge need for AWS certification and that the human resources available for this type of skill are insufficient. Therefore, it's better to learn these skills now than to compete the next time.

With the rapid expansion of digitization and the IoT (thanks in particular to the smartphone industry), the area of cloud consumption is truly huge. Big enough to withstand its competitors. Since it depends on the consumer, you prefer at least one trial on AWS, which appears to be attractive enough to be accepted by consumers forever. Today's long-tail use case could reach the size of the entire cloud computing market in 2017 in the next 10-12 years - Google, Digital Ocean, and Microsoft are well-positioned to take advantage of Amazon's offerings. However, in terms of "time required", AWS has a better advantage over these competitors.

With the growing wings, in which AWS Nokia has already shaken hands for 5G, IoT, and cloud services, it has attracted the attention and confidence of cloud customers/service providers. Due to the seriousness of the results, employees are ready to work with AWS. In addition to the goodwill rights, AWS can also meet modern cloud service requirements. It provides its clients with access to a full set of virtual computers at any time via the Internet. For this reason, AWS Cloud Services, with its double error, will overshadow its peers and extend its approach over time.

In practice, a company will only need more than one server if it has users who cannot host it. Given the cost savings, we could also consider maximizing profit margins, and here AWS will play an important role.

Given the increasing enlightenment of cloud computing and associated costs, companies will naturally reduce their prices to face competition, but for what purpose? You also need to maintain the brand value (as before). They also offer services offered by AWS at relatively higher prices. In this case, the consumer will ultimately benefit from the limited competition and the search for a dominant position. Prices will be so low that cloud services will be cheaper than Internet connections. If the infrastructure were not as high as the demand we see today, consumers themselves would face a crisis.

I hope you have learned something!

CPSIA information can be obtained
at www.ICGtesting.com
Printed in the USA
BVHW071336090321
602012BV00009B/1774